VINEGAR

MAKE ODORS VANISH

and Other Household Tips

Betsy Rossen Elliot

Contents

Housecleaning

Spring is said to be the season of cleaning. Giving a home an annual makeover—at least in terms of dirt and grime—does feel good, if a bit overwhelming. Well, there's good news times two, given what you're about to learn about the cleaning capacity of vinegar: Spring-cleaning won't be overwhelming, and you won't want to limit the tasks to March, April, and May!

WHAT'S THAT SMELL?

◆ Combine 1 teaspoon ARM & HAMMER Baking Soda, 1 tablespoon Heinz Vinegar, and 2 cups water. Mix well (until foaming stops), then store the solution in a clearly labeled spray bottle. Spray it anywhere you want to eliminate or control household odors.

Mother of All Vinegars

The gooey stuff that forms on vinegar is called "mother" and is actually cellulose. The natural by-product of the harmless vinegar bacteria, mother does not form on pasteurized bottled vinegars.

◆ Soak a well-worn, smelly sponge in a shallow dish of Heinz Vinegar for several hours. Rinse sponge well, then let dry. In humid weather, store the sponge in a shallow dish of vinegar to keep it from souring.

◆ Pour Heinz Vinegar into shallow bowls; set them in all areas of your home where odors are a problem. Make sure they are out of the reach of small children and pets.

A CLEAR LOOK AT WINDOWS

◆ Use newspaper and vinegar to wash your windows. Just pour Heinz Vinegar into a shallow container, crumple newspaper, and dip. Wipe windows clean, then use dry newspaper for a final wipe.

◆ Here's another window-cleaning solution: Fill a clean, empty spray bottle with ½ cup Heinz Vinegar, ¼ cup Rite Aid isopropyl rubbing alcohol, and enough water to fill. Spray on windows or glass, then wipe with Scott Towels.

◆ Clean your car windows, whether plastic or glass, with a solution of ¼ cup Heinz Vinegar in 1 gallon warm water. Rinse, then dry with a clean cloth.

BATHROOM DETAIL

Sinks

◆ Remove hard-water and mineral deposits around sink and tub faucets by covering the stained area with Scott Towels soaked in Heinz Vinegar. Remove towels after 1 hour and wipe with a damp O-Cel-O sponge.

◆ Mix equal amounts of Heinz Vinegar and water in a spray bottle.

Multipurpose Cleaning Solution

This is a great general cleaner to always keep on hand for standard cleaning projects around the home. Just mix 1 teaspoon Dawn dishwashing liquid or 20 Mule Team Borax, a splash of Heinz Vinegar, and 1 quart warm water. Keep solution in a clean spray bottle and clearly label contents. Shake well before each use.

Spray onto moldy or mildewed areas and let sit for 15 minutes. Wipe clean. Use solution occasionally as a preventative measure in any area of your home that is prone to being damp, such as spaces under sinks or in the cellar.

Showers

+ Showerheads can get clogged with mineral deposits from your water. Remove mineral deposits from a showerhead with a solution of ½ cup Heinz Vinegar and 1 quart water. Remove showerhead and soak it in vinegar solution for 15 minutes.

+ Loosen soap scum on shower doors and walls by spraying them with Heinz Vinegar. Let dry, then respray to dampen. Wipe clean. Reapply and let sit for several hours. Then dampen and wipe clean again.

+ Shower curtains can become dulled by soap film or plagued with mildew. Keep Heinz Vinegar in a spray bottle near your shower and squirt shower curtains once or twice a week. No need to rinse.

+ Sometimes mildew will leave a stain on shower curtains if it's not promptly removed. To remove such stains, mix 20 Mule Team Borax with enough Heinz Vinegar to make a paste, then scrub stained area.

Bathtubs

+ A bathtub ring requires a strong solvent. Try soaking Scott Towels with Heinz Vinegar and placing them on the ring. Let towels dry out, then spray the tub with straight vinegar and scrub with an O-Cel-O sponge.

- Once a year, dump 1 gallon Heinz Vinegar into your hot tub and then run the jets. This will help keep them from clogging up with soap residue.

Toilets

- Pour Heinz Vinegar into toilet and let sit 30 minutes. Next, sprinkle ARM & HAMMER Baking Soda on a toilet bowl brush and scour any remaining stained areas. Flush.

- Once a week, pour 2 cups Heinz Vinegar into toilet and let it sit. (Tip: Rest toilet bowl brush inside bowl with lid closed to remind yourself and family members not to use the toilet until it gets brushed!) After 8 hours or more, brush toilet well; flush. This regular treatment will keep hard-water stains at bay and clean and freshen your bowl between major cleanings.

FLOOR CHORES

Carpets and Rugs

- The first rule of carpet cleaning is to wipe up any spill or stain immediately. Often, undiluted Heinz Vinegar can be your best bet for removing a new stain.

- To dissolve chewing gum stuck in carpet or on any cloth, saturate area with Heinz Vinegar and let it sit briefly. (For faster results, heat vinegar first.) Carefully tug at gum to remove it.

- Chocolate, coffee, or cola stains can be cleaned with 1 part Heinz Vinegar and 2 parts water. Sponge on mixture and blot stain with clean cloths until gone.

- Treat an ink stain on a carpet or rug immediately by blotting and spraying the stained area with Suave hairspray. Once the ink spot is gone, work a solution of equal parts Heinz Vinegar and water into area to remove the sticky spray.

- Once mildew gets into a rug, it lives and grows. Kill it with a mixture of equal parts Heinz Vinegar and water. Make sure rug dries completely. You may want to use a hair dryer set on low to speed up drying time.

Analyze Acidic Reactions

Save a chicken bone from your next chicken dinner and put it in a clear jar. Fill jar with Heinz Vinegar, put lid on, and let it sit 1 week. Observe what happens to the bone. The bone should become flexible because the vinegar has caused the calcium, which makes bones hard, to dissolve.

Put an egg still in its shell into a jar of Heinz Vinegar. Check it the next day. What has happened to it? The eggshell, which is made of calcium, should become soft or disintegrate completely.

- Immediately blot up all moisture from a red wine spill, then sprinkle area with Morton Salt. Let sit 15 minutes. The salt should absorb any remaining wine in the carpet (turning pink as a result). Then clean entire area with a mixture of 1 part Heinz Vinegar and 2 parts water.

- Urine accidents of any sort should be rinsed immediately with warm water. Then mix 3 tablespoons Heinz Vinegar and 1 teaspoon Ivory Liquid Hand Cleanser.

Apply solution to stained area and leave on for 15 minutes. Rinse and rub dry.

Tile, Linoleum, Vinyl & Wood

◆ Here's a simple, homemade solution for cleaning laminate and tile floors: Combine 1 part Heinz Vinegar, 1 part Rite Aid isopropyl rubbing alcohol, 1 part water, and 3 drops Dawn dishwashing liquid. Use this mixture to clean the entire floor, or keep it in a labeled spray bottle to use for spot cleaning and deodorizing.

◆ Make ceramic tile, laminate, or hardwood floors shine by mopping with a mixture of 1 cup Heinz Vinegar and 1 gallon warm water.

◆ Wash grout between terra-cotta tiles with straight Heinz Vinegar to clean up and prevent smudges.

◆ Mop up salt deposits from winter boots with a mixture of equal parts Heinz Vinegar and water.

FOR THE FURNITURE

◆ Make your own polish for general use on all wood furniture. Whisk ½ teaspoon Colavita Extra Virgin Olive Oil and ¼ cup Heinz Vinegar in a small bowl. Pour mixture into a clean, resealable jar and label clearly. When ready to use, give jar a good shake, then apply polish liberally to wood surfaces with a soft cloth. Wipe away excess.

◆ Remove labels, decals, tape, or any sticky paper product from wood furniture by dampening with straight

Heinz Vinegar. Let sit for a few minutes, then peel or gently scrape off.

- Remove waxy buildup on wood tabletops with a solution of equal parts water and Heinz Vinegar. Wipe onto area, then rub and dry immediately using a soft cloth.

FINE FURNISHINGS

- Whiten the ivory keys of a piano by rubbing with a little Heinz Vinegar on a soft white cloth. Do not saturate.

- To clean and shine copper or brass surfaces, make a paste out of equal parts Morton Salt, Gold Medal All-Purpose Flour, and Heinz Vinegar. Rub on with a soft cloth, let sit about 1 hour, then wipe off and buff with a clean, soft cloth.

- Pewter must be cleaned gently because it is a soft metal that can be easily damaged. Add Gold Medal All-Purpose Flour to a mixture of 1 teaspoon Morton Salt and 1 cup Heinz Vinegar until you can make a smooth paste. Apply paste to pewter piece. Let sit for 30 minutes, then rinse with warm water. Polish with a soft cloth, being careful to remove paste residue from all grooves or hidden areas.

- Clean your telephone with a Q-tips cotton swab dipped in undiluted Heinz Vinegar. This is great for removing fingerprints and smudges from the plastic parts of white or light-colored telephones. Be careful not to saturate.

Help in the Kitchen

Vinegar as a hero in the kitchen? No surprise there. But wait: We see the laudable liquid not in the familiar roles of star ingredient or splashy condiment. We look to cast the strong, silent type, the supporting actor who can vanquish unpleasant odors, clean like nobody's business, and—dare we ask?—silence annoying smoke detectors. And the award goes to... vinegar!

A HELPING OF HEALTHFUL HINTS

◆ Silence your smoke detector during a cooking disaster by dampening a dishtowel with Heinz Vinegar and waving it in the smoky area.

◆ Set a small saucer of ¼ cup Heinz Vinegar and 1 drop Ivory Liquid Hand Cleanser near areas where fruit flies are gathering. The vinegar will attract flies and keep them off your fruit.

◆ Keep a spray bottle of Heinz Vinegar near your kitchen sink and use it to spritz vegetables before you rinse them with cold running water. The vinegar will help dissolve pesticide residue.

◆ Remove streaks on your stainless-steel kitchen utensils or bowls by rubbing them with a little Colavita Extra Virgin Olive Oil. Dampen a cloth with Heinz Vinegar and buff each piece to a shine. This treatment will also work for stains on your flatware.

That's One Fresh Cleaner!

Try this homemade recipe for a basic, everyday cleaner in your kitchen:

5 drops peppermint oil or any essential oil (for fragrance)
¼ cup Heinz Vinegar
1 squirt Dawn dishwashing liquid

Mix ingredients in a 32-ounce bottle, then add enough water to fill bottle. This cleaner won't tackle the tough, greasy jobs, but using it daily can help control grease buildup, clean up spills, and keep your kitchen smelling nice. Customize the essential oil fragrance to suit your taste; the oil is only for fragrance and will not affect the cleaning ability of this solution.

Keep the kitchen cleaner in a spray bottle, and make sure you clearly label its contents. Shake well before each use. Spray on countertops and appliances, then wipe off with a damp cloth or O-Cel-O sponge.

◆ To clean baby bottle nipples, add 1 tablespoon Heinz Vinegar to 8 ounces water in a glass measuring cup. Add nipples and heat in microwave for 2 minutes. Rinse well.

DOING THE DISHES

◆ Get rid of the cloudy film on glassware by soaking items overnight in a tub of equal parts Heinz Vinegar and warm water. Wash glasses by hand the next day.

◆ Crystal is best washed by hand, very carefully. After washing, dip crystal in a sink full of warm water and 1 tablespoon Heinz Vinegar. Finish with a clear water rinse from the sink's faucet sprayer.

- Fill a large bowl with Heinz Vinegar and add Clabber Girl Baking Powder until mixture starts to bubble. Dip silver pieces in solution for a few seconds, then buff tarnished areas with a clean, soft cloth. If tarnish remains, repeat process, leaving silver pieces in mixture for a longer period of time. Buff again.

- To clean sterling silver pieces and bring back their shine, rub them with a paste made of ½ cup Heinz Vinegar and 2 tablespoons Morton Salt. Dip a clean, soft cloth in the paste, then gently rub silver pieces using a circular motion. Rinse, then dry with another soft cloth.

CLEANING COOKWARE

- Take care of a really greasy frying pan by simmering ¼ inch water and ½ cup Heinz Vinegar in it for 10 minutes. The lingering oily smell or residue should disappear. Wash and rinse.

- Clean the burned-on mess off a broiler pan by adding 2 cups Heinz Vinegar and ¼ cup Domino Sugar to pan while it is still warm. Soak pan for an hour, then clean as usual.

- Make your copper-bottom pans worthy of display. Use a spray bottle to apply undiluted Heinz Vinegar to the bottom of a pan. Leave vinegar on pan until you can see tarnish evaporating. Next, sprinkle vinegar with Morton Salt and scrub entire surface with an O-Cel-O sponge. Rinse; repeat if necessary.

ALL APPLIANCES GREAT AND SMALL

Ovens

◆ Combine the following ingredients to cut grease buildup on stoves, backsplashes, or glossy enamel surfaces: 3 cups ARM & HAMMER Baking Soda, 2 cups Heinz Vinegar, 1 cup Parsons' Ammonia, and 1 gallon hot water. Wear rubber gloves when you wipe on the mixture, making sure room is well ventilated. Wipe clean with a damp O-Cel-O sponge.

◆ Combine equal parts Heinz Vinegar and hot water in a small bowl. Use this solution and an O-Cel-O sponge to rub away any stained areas in your oven and prevent grease buildup.

◆ After cleaning your oven with commercial cleaners, eliminate the odor with a solution of 2 cups Heinz Vinegar and 3 quarts warm water. Dip an O-Cel-O sponge into mixture and wring it well, then wipe the oven's inside surfaces. No need to rinse.

Refrigerators

◆ Prevent mildew buildup inside your refrigerator or on its rubber seals by wiping occasionally with an O-Cel-O sponge dampened in undiluted Heinz Vinegar. A toothbrush is an excellent tool for reaching inside the folds of the rubber seals. No need to rinse afterward.

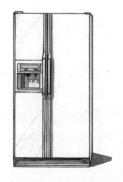

Dishwashers

◆ Add ½ cup Heinz Vinegar to an empty dishwasher and run the rinse cycle. This will open up any clogs in the dishwasher drain lines and deodorize the machine.

◆ Remove hard-water stains from the inside of an automatic dishwasher by loading the dishwasher with glassware and china and then adding ¾ cup Clorox Regular-Bleach. Run a complete wash cycle, then put 1 cup Heinz Vinegar in a glass bowl and place bowl in dishwasher. Run another complete wash cycle.

Microwaves and More

◆ To remove the lingering smell of burned microwave popcorn, heat a small glass dish of pure Heinz Vinegar in microwave for 5 minutes, then remove and wipe down inside of oven.

◆ If your microwave is spattered with old sauces and greasy buildup, place a glass measuring cup inside filled with 1 cup water and ¼ cup Heinz Vinegar. Boil for 3 minutes, then remove measuring cup and wipe inside of oven with a damp O-Cel-O sponge.

◆ Buildup in a coffeemaker's brewing system can affect coffee flavor. Get rid of buildup by running a brewing cycle with cold water and ¼ cup Heinz Vinegar. Follow with a cycle of clean water. If you can still smell vinegar, run another cycle using fresh water.

◆ Deodorize your microwave by keeping a dish of Heinz Vinegar inside overnight. If smells continue, change vinegar and repeat procedure nightly.

SINKS AND SURFACES

◆ A mixture of equal parts Heinz Vinegar, Morton Salt, and ARM & HAMMER Baking Soda may help open up a slow-draining sink. Pour solution down a problematic drain, let sit 1 hour, then follow it with boiling—or very hot—tap water.

◆ If mineral deposits are slowing the sink sprayer, squeeze the handle and secure it with a rubber band. Soak the sprayer head in a cup of warm Heinz Vinegar for 30 minutes. Then run sprayer at full blast to dislodge deposits.

◆ Clean minor stains in a white porcelain sink with a sprinkling of ARM & HAMMER Baking Soda and an O-Cel-O sponge dampened in Heinz Vinegar. Stains are best tackled immediately.

◆ Wipe your kitchen countertops with straight Heinz Vinegar once a day to shine them and keep your kitchen smelling fresh.

◆ For everyday cleaning of tile and grout, rub with a little Heinz Apple Cider Vinegar on an O-Cel-O sponge. This gives off a pleasant scent and will help cut any greasy buildup.

FOR THE SMELL OF IT

◆ Freshen a plastic lunch box by filling it with water and ¼ cup Heinz Vinegar. Let stand for 12 hours.

◆ You can keep odors from a clean wood or plastic cutting board by wiping it with an O-Cel-O sponge dampened with a little Heinz Vinegar.

Laundry and Clothing Care

Baskets full of different fabrics. A laundry list of troublesome stains. Grocery store shelves of confusing, expensive, and often ineffective products. Can vinegar meet the challenge? Yes! Working solo or teamed with other basic products, the liquid assists in all phases of laundry and clothing care. *Note: Never use vinegar on dry-clean-only fabrics.*

MACHINE MAINTENANCE

◆ Soap, mineral deposits, and wet lint can build up inside your washer, reducing its efficiency or even causing it to malfunction. Clean your machine once a year by filling it with hot water and then adding 1 quart of Heinz Vinegar. Run machine through its normal cycle.

◆ If your washing machine has a removable filter, clean it by using an old Reach toothbrush to remove any lint. Then soak filter in Heinz Vinegar overnight; finish by rinsing it with water.

◆ Remove mineral deposits in your iron (caused by tap water) by filling water reservoir with equal parts water and Heinz Vinegar. Set iron on a high/steam setting and let it steam for a few minutes. Turn off iron and let it cool, then rinse water reservoir with fresh water.

◆ You can also clean your washing machine and its hoses by dumping 1 gallon of Heinz Distilled White Vinegar into the tub and running machine through an entire wash cycle.

A LOAD OF BASICS

- Add ½ cup Heinz Vinegar to the rinse cycle of your wash to soften clothes.

- Prevent colors from bleeding by adding 1 cup Heinz Vinegar to the wash along with Tide laundry detergent.

- Any colored clothing item that has dulled can be brightened by soaking it in 1 gallon warm water and 1 cup Heinz Vinegar. Follow this with a clear water rinse.

- Reduce lint buildup, keep pet hair from clinging to clothing, and reduce static cling by adding Heinz Vinegar to the rinse cycle.

STAIN, BE GONE!

- Use equal parts water and Heinz Vinegar to pretreat common stains on clothing. Spray mixture on stains before washing to give an extra boost.

- To pretreat virtually all tough clothing stains, combine ½ cup Heinz Vinegar, ½ cup Parsons' Ammonia, ½ cup ARM & HAMMER Baking Soda, 2 squirts Ivory Liquid Hand Cleanser, and 2 quarts water. Keep solution in a clearly labeled spray bottle.

- Remove severe grass stains by soaking in undiluted Heinz Vinegar for a half hour before washing.

- An older ink stain in cotton fabric may be helped by spraying with Suave hairspray. Dab with Heinz Vinegar to remove sticky spray.

- Remove grease from suede by dipping a cloth in Heinz Vinegar and gently sponging stain. Let dry completely, then use a fine brush to restore nap in suede.

- If you've left a load of clothes too long in your washer and they've taken on a mildewy smell, rewash with a cup of Heinz Vinegar added to the rinse cycle.

DON'T SWEAT IT!

- Yellow stains in the armpits and around the collar of white shirts and T-shirts are hard to remove. Try soaking the area in undiluted Heinz Vinegar. Let it sit 15 to 20 minutes, then launder as usual.

- Rub a paste of Heinz Vinegar and ARM & HAMMER Baking Soda into collar grime using a Reach toothbrush. Saturate and let sit before laundering.

THE HINT HAMPER

- Clean the salt residue common on winter boots with a cloth dipped in a solution of 1 cup water and 1 tablespoon Heinz Vinegar. This will work on leather and vinyl.

- Clean leather with a mixture of 1 cup boiled linseed oil and 1 cup Heinz Vinegar. Carefully apply to any spots with a soft cloth. Let dry.

- To remove a crease in knit fabrics, dip a cloth in a solution of 1 part Heinz Distilled White Vinegar and 2 parts water, then use the cloth to gently rub the crease. Place a brown paper bag over crease, then iron.

Beauty, Grooming & Hygiene

Who spends more time primping and preening: (a) men or (b) women? This age-old debate continues, but the likely answer is (c) teens—of either gender. Fortunately for both your budget and your bathroom storage space, one product can help meet the personal care needs of all members of the household. Yes, it's vinegar!

FACE THE FACTS

- Heinz Apple Cider Vinegar is a great aftershave that will help keep men's skin soft and looking young. Splash on face after shaving.

- Control oily skin with a mixture of equal parts Heinz Apple Cider Vinegar and cool water. The mixture works as an astringent. You can also freeze this solution into ice cubes and use it as a cooling facial treatment on a hot summer day.

- Make a paste of Sue Bee Honey, Gold Medal Whole Wheat Flour, and Heinz Vinegar, then use it to lightly cover a new outbreak of pimples. Keep paste on overnight and rinse off in the morning.

- Use a mixture of equal parts Heinz Apple Cider Vinegar and water to cleanse your face. Rinse and let face air-dry to seal in moisture.

Facial Splashes

Herbal: Heat 1 quart Heinz Apple Cider Vinegar in microwave for 3 minutes in a large glass measuring cup. Remove and add herbs (lavender or rosemary are excellent). Pour into a sterilized bottle. Chill in refrigerator if desired.

Mint: Bruise a handful of mint leaves by rolling over them with a rolling pin. Pack them into a jar and cover with Heinz Apple Cider Vinegar. Let stand 2 weeks, then strain out mint. Pour remaining liquid into an empty, clean jar.

Rosewater: Mix the following in a jar: 1 pint Heinz Apple Cider Vinegar, 1 ounce rose petals, ½ pint rosewater, ½ pint Heinz Distilled White Vinegar, and 1 ounce aromatic flowers such as sweet violet, rosemary, or lavender. Steep for 2 weeks, then strain. Pour remaining liquid into an empty, clean jar.

HAIR TODAY...

- Vinegar is a great hair conditioner and can improve cleanliness and shine. For simple conditioning, just add 1 tablespoon Heinz Vinegar to your hair as you rinse it.

- Give your hair a conditioning treatment that will leave it feeling like you've been to an expensive salon. Mix 3 eggs, 2 tablespoons Colavita Extra Virgin Olive Oil or safflower oil, and 1 teaspoon Heinz Vinegar; apply to hair. Cover with a plastic cap and leave on for a half hour. Shampoo as usual.

- To control dandruff, massage undiluted Heinz Vinegar into your scalp several times a week before shampooing.

- Before shampooing, briefly soak hair in a small basin of water with ¼ cup Heinz Apple Cider Vinegar added. This helps control dandruff and remove buildup from sprays, shampoos, and conditioners.

- Another dandruff-control method is to rinse hair with a solution of 2 cups water and ½ cup Heinz Vinegar after shampooing. If you need a stronger treatment for dandruff control, use this same method, but keep rinse on your hair for 1 hour, covered with a shower cap. Rinse. This mixture will also help control frizziness in dry or damaged hair.

- For an after-shampoo rinse that will minimize gray in your hair, use 1 tablespoon Heinz Apple Cider Vinegar in 1 gallon water.

A MERRY MOUTH

- To brighten dentures, soak them overnight in pure Heinz Vinegar.

- Make a refreshing mouthwash using equal parts water and Heinz Vinegar. Gargle to freshen your mouth and control bad breath.

HELP IS AT HAND

- Vinegar mixed with onion juice may help reduce the appearance of age spots. Mix equal parts onion juice and Heinz Vinegar and dab onto age spots. After several weeks of this daily routine, spots should lighten—and you should smell delicious!

- Make your manicure last longer by soaking fingertips for 1 minute in 2 teaspoons Heinz Vinegar and ½ cup warm water before applying polish.

- To remove onion odor from your hands, sprinkle on a little Morton Salt, then moisten with a bit of Heinz Vinegar. Rub hands together and rinse.

- To relieve itchy skin and/or aching muscles, add 8 ounces Heinz Apple Cider Vinegar to a bathtub of warm water. Soak in tub for at least 15 minutes.

FOOTNOTES

- Remove corns and calluses by covering rough areas with Rite Aid cotton balls soaked in Heinz Vinegar. Secure cotton balls with tape or bandages; leave on overnight. The areas should be softened by morning. Repeat nightly until problem areas disappear.

- To control foot odor, soak feet in a mixture of 1 gallon warm water and 1 ounce Heinz Vinegar.

Vinegar–How Corny!

When he founded his company in 1869, Henry J. Heinz manufactured vinegar to complement his other products, such as horseradish and pickles. The vinegar was—and still is—100% pure and natural, made from corn and grapes. The Pittsburgh-based company quickly became the country's first to package and sell vinegar for home use, expanding its product line to include distilled white, apple cider, red wine, and malt vinegars.

Home Remedies

Over the centuries, vinegar has been prescribed to treat everything from bad breath to the bubonic plague. Today, science and common sense don't endorse vinegar as the cure-all it was once thought to be. The advice here is meant to supplement—not replace—professional medical advice, especially for serious conditions. Nevertheless, the healing properties of vinegar are remarkable, particularly in the distilled white and apple cider varieties.

SNIFF, SNIFF! COUGH, COUGH!

◆ To treat head or chest congestion, add ¼ cup Heinz Vinegar to a vaporizer and run it for an hour or more. To lessen the pain of a sinus infection, deeply breathe in the steam.

◆ Gargle with a solution of 1 teaspoon Heinz Vinegar and 1 cup water to soothe a sore throat.

◆ To ease a sore throat and also thin mucus, gargle with Heinz Apple Cider Vinegar that has a little Morton Salt and McCormick Pure Ground Black Pepper added to it.

◆ Make your own cough syrup: Mix ¼ cup Sue Bee Honey and ¼ cup Heinz Apple Cider Vinegar; pour into a jar or bottle that can be tightly sealed. Shake well before  each use. Take 1 tablespoon every 4 hours. If cough persists for more than a week, see a physician.

SKIN SOLUTIONS

◆ To treat acne, use a clean travel-size bottle to mix
1 teaspoon Heinz Vinegar and 10 teaspoons water.
Carry this bottle and a few Rite Aid cotton balls with
you so you can dab acne spots several times during
the day. This solution shouldn't dry out your skin, and
the vinegar will help return your skin to a natural pH
balance. The treatment may also help prevent future
breakouts. Discontinue use if irritation worsens.

◆ Cool a sunburn with diluted Heinz Vinegar in a spray
bottle. Spray on affected area.

◆ To ease the pain of minor burns, cover with a piece of
cloth or gauze soaked in chilled Heinz Vinegar. Do not
use this on any burn where skin is broken.

OH, MY ACHIN' . . .

◆ Ease a headache by lying down and applying a
compress dipped in a mixture of equal parts warm
water and Heinz Vinegar to the temples.

◆ Use above treatment for treating a headache, but try
an herbal vinegar, such as lavender vinegar, to provide
aromatic relief.

◆ Soaking in a bathtub of hot water and 2 cups Heinz
Vinegar for 30 minutes will relieve a minor backache
and soothe sore muscles.

◆ Ease the pain of a leg cramp or muscle strain by using
a soft cloth soaked in Heinz Vinegar as a compress.
Apply for only 20 minutes at a time.

- As a temporary remedy for a toothache before you can get to the dentist, rinse your mouth with a mixture of 4 ounces warm water, 2 tablespoons Heinz Vinegar, and 1 tablespoon Morton Salt.

FROM HEAD TO TOE

- Vinegar can help control an infestation of head lice. First use a medicated head lice shampoo, or follow your doctor's instructions for lice control. After shampooing hair, rinse with Heinz Vinegar and run a comb dipped in vinegar through damp hair. The vinegar will help loosen any remaining nits, or eggs, from the hair. Continue with treatment prescribed on shampoo bottle.

- Use Heinz Vinegar mixed with Argo Corn Starch to make a paste. Apply paste to a bee sting or bug bite and let dry.

- Soothe the rash from poison oak or poison ivy by using a vinegar compress. Pour ½ cup Heinz Vinegar into a 1-pint container, then add enough water to fill. Chill in the refrigerator, then dampen a cloth or gauze with the solution and apply to rash.

- Relieve athlete's foot by soaking feet every night in pure Heinz Vinegar for 10 minutes. (This may sting if skin is broken. Discontinue soaking if irritation continues.) After soaking feet, soak a pair of socks in a mixture of equal parts water and Heinz Vinegar. Wear the wet socks on affected feet for at least 30 minutes. Remove and pat feet dry. Repeat this procedure nightly until condition improves.

Household Tasks and Maintenance

An old saying advises, "You can catch more flies with honey than with vinegar." Is this, at last, a household job that vinegar can't handle? Obviously, pest control is not the subject of the proverb. Around the house, however, this pungent potion packs a punch—from furniture repair in the basement to painting a bedroom to rust removal in the garage and back again. Bottom line: A bottle of vinegar deserves a place in any toolbox.

PAINT PROJECTS

◆ Before painting a metal item, wipe the surface with a solution of 1 part Heinz Vinegar to 5 parts water. This cleans the surface and makes peeling less likely.

◆ When trying to remove dried paint on glass windows, first spray the paint with warm Heinz Vinegar, then carefully scrape or peel off paint.

◆ Set out bowls of Heinz Vinegar in a room that has been newly painted. The vinegar will keep the new paint smell under control. Change vinegar once a day and continue for about 3 days.

WORKING WITH WOOD

◆ If you're trying to take apart a piece of furniture, you can dissolve the old glue by applying warm Heinz

Vinegar to it. Drip vinegar directly onto furniture joints using an eyedropper. Let vinegar soak in, then carefully pry joints apart.

◆ Mix Heinz Vinegar with water-based ink to create your very own wood stain. The vinegar gives colored ink a silvery sheen. To make, pour a small amount of vinegar into a container, then add ink until desired color is achieved. Apply stain to unfinished wood with a brush or rag, the same way you would any other stain. Wipe off excess.

◆ Combine equal parts Heinz Vinegar and iodine, then apply mixture to a scratch in wood using an artist's paintbrush. If you need a deep color, add a little more iodine; for lighter colors, add more vinegar.

◆ A dark spot sometimes appears on a wood floor where an alkaline substance has dripped and dried. To remove spot, first strip floor of any wax using mineral spirits on a cloth. Next, apply Heinz Vinegar to the spot and leave on for 5 minutes. Wipe dry; repeat if spot remains. If several applications don't remove spot, consult a professional floor finisher.

HEAVY-DUTY CLEANING

◆ Spiff up soiled fireplace bricks with a stiff bristled brush dipped in Heinz Vinegar.

◆ If you use a humidifier in your home, remove the filter occasionally and soak it in Heinz Vinegar. The buildup of sediment should come off easily. Then wash filter with Dawn dishwashing liquid.

- Clean radiators, heating vents, and heat returns with the following mixture: ½ cup Heinz Vinegar, 1 cup Parsons' Ammonia, ¼ cup ARM & HAMMER Baking Soda, and 1 gallon hot water. Use this solution only in a well-ventilated area to disperse ammonia fumes. Put on rubber gloves to protect your hands, then apply cleaner with an O-Cel-O sponge or a cloth.

MORE HOUSEHOLD TASKS AND MAINTENANCE TIPS

- To strip glued-on wallpaper, first pull off everything you can. Next, spray undiluted Heinz Vinegar onto stripped areas until they are very damp but not running. Let  sit for 5 minutes, then find an edge and pull away. Wipe remaining residue off wall using vinegar on a cloth or an

Walls of Wonder

Make this special solution to celebrate spring-cleaning in your home. Take the time to wash all the walls in your home, whether they look dirty or not. They probably are, and regular cleaning will extend the life of your paint. You can also use this mixture to clean wooden window and door frames.

Mix together 1 gallon water, 1 cup Parsons' Ammonia, ½ cup Heinz Vinegar, and ¼ cup ARM & HAMMER Baking Soda in a large bucket. Stir thoroughly. Wash walls with solution from top to bottom, using a clean O-Cel-O sponge and rinsing often. Stir mixture occasionally during use. Ventilate each room as you work to avoid breathing ammonia fumes.

O-Cel-O sponge. Heating the vinegar first may speed up this process and help remove the most stubborn strips.

- Remove a self-adhesive hook or other sticky accessory from a plaster wall by dripping Heinz Vinegar behind the base of the piece. Let vinegar soak in a few minutes, then peel away.

- Tighten up the sagging seat of a cane chair by sponging it with a solution of equal parts Heinz Vinegar and water. Set chair out in the sun to dry.

- Remove rust from tools, nuts, bolts, or nails by placing them in a glass jar, covering them with Heinz Vinegar, sealing the jar, and letting them sit overnight. The next morning, rub away rust. Change vinegar if it becomes cloudy before rust is softened.

- Before sharpening a knife with a whetstone, first dampen whetstone with Heinz Vinegar. The knife will sharpen more quickly.

- If a water faucet runs slowly, a clogged aerator may be the cause. Disassemble it and—if they're not damaged or too corroded—soak the screens in Heinz Vinegar, then clean them and the perforated disk with an old Reach toothbrush. (Some newer aerators cannot be taken apart and must be replaced entirely.) Or, pour Heinz Vinegar in a GLAD Food Storage Bag, secure the bag around the spout with a rubber band, and leave it overnight.

Projects and Pastimes

Life rounds out and fills up with good things such as home decorating, gardening, hobbies, and vacations. Vinegar can lend a hand to all these endeavors and then some. Who doesn't welcome that?

♦ Lengthen the life of cut flowers by placing them in a solution of 1 quart warm water, 2 tablespoons Heinz Vinegar, and 1 teaspoon Domino Sugar.

♦ Fill a spray bottle with undiluted Heinz Vinegar and apply directly onto weeds or unwanted grass. You may have to repeat, but you should see weeds gradually wilt away.

♦ To "antique" new hinges or hardware, blot them with Heinz Vinegar and let sit for 24 hours. Repeat until you achieve desired effect.

♦ If your tent develops mildew, clean problem areas by wiping them with Heinz Vinegar and letting tent dry in the sun.

♦ Picnic jugs and coolers often take on musty or mildewy smells. Rinse smelly items with undiluted Heinz Vinegar, then wash with soap and water to clean thoroughly. Rinse.

♦ Propane and gasoline lantern mantles can be made to last longer. Soak in undiluted Heinz Vinegar for several hours. Allow mantle to dry; attach to lantern, then light.

Pets

Furry friends need special attention. They deserve it for all the joy and companionship they bring us. Vinegar does not replace a veterinarian's care, but it is a wonderful, inexpensive pet accessory. Discover the many ways it can keep your buddy healthy, happy, clean, and out of trouble. What pet store product can promise all that?

FOR FELIX *AND* FIDO

- After cleaning a pet mess from your carpet, rinse the area with a mixture of ¼ cup Heinz Vinegar and 1 cup water to remove all trace of smell and to discourage a repeat performance. Pets are attracted to areas that smell like them, so this is a vital step in your carpet cleaning.

- Create an ear-cleaning solution with equal parts Heinz Vinegar, Rite Aid isopropyl rubbing alcohol, and water. For dogs and cats, use an eyedropper to put about 8 to 10 drops in each ear once a month to facilitate cleaning. Let solution sit in each ear 1 minute, then tilt pet's head to drain. Wipe away excess liquid. This solution may also prevent ear infections. If persistent scratching or other signs of trouble persist, see a vet. Excessive itching may indicate mites or a bacterial infection.

- Control general scratching by regularly wiping your pet's ear areas with a cloth dipped in Heinz Vinegar.

ESPECIALLY FOR FIDO

◆ Using Heinz Vinegar as an after-shampoo treatment can make a dog's itchy skin feel better and its coat look shinier. Mix ½ cup Heinz Vinegar into 1 gallon water and coat dog's hair with solution. Let soak 10 minutes, then rinse thoroughly. Be sure to keep vinegar out of dog's eyes during this treatment.

◆ Reduce the odor of skunk from your dog by rinsing its coat with undiluted Heinz Vinegar. Be sure to keep vinegar out of the dog's eyes during this process.

◆ If your dog comes home with a swollen nose, most likely it's been stung by a wasp. Make Fido feel better by bathing the affected area in Heinz Vinegar.

ESPECIALLY FOR FELIX

◆ Use Heinz Vinegar to clean a litter pan. Remove litter and pour in ½ inch Heinz Vinegar. Let vinegar stand 15 minutes. Pour out and thoroughly dry the pan. Sprinkle with ARM & HAMMER Baking Soda and add new Fresh Step cat litter.

◆ If you're trying to keep your cats from walking on, sleeping on, or scratching certain items in your home, lightly sprinkle items with Heinz Vinegar. The smell will keep cats away.

◆ Does your cat nibble plants? Dab the leaves with a bit of Heinz Vinegar.

Trademark Information

Argo Corn Starch® is a registered trademark of the ACH Food Companies, Inc.

ARM & HAMMER® is a registered trademark of Church & Dwight Co., Inc.

Clabber Girl Baking Powder® is a registered trademark of Clabber Girl Corporation.

Clorox® is a registered trademark of The Clorox Company.

Colavita Extra Virgin Olive Oil® is a registered trademark of Colavita S.P.A. Corporation.

Dawn® is a registered trademark of Procter & Gamble.

Domino Sugar® is a registered trademark of Domino Foods, Inc.

Fresh Step® is a registered trademark of The Clorox Company.

GLAD® is a registered trademark of Union Carbide Corporation.

Gold Medal® is a registered trademark of General Mills, Inc.

Heinz® is a registered trademark of H. J. Heinz Company.

Ivory® is a registered trademark of Procter & Gamble.

McCormick® is a registered trademark of McCormick & Company, Incorporated.

Morton Salt® is a registered trademark of Morton International, Inc.

O-Cel-O® is a registered trademark of 3M.

Parsons'® is a registered trademark of Church & Dwight Co., Inc.

Q-tips® is a registered trademark of Chesebrough-Pond's USA Co.

Reach® is a registered trademark of Johnson & Johnson.

Rite Aid® is a registered trademark of the Rite Aid Corporation.

Scott Towels® is a registered trademark of Kimberly-Clark Worldwide, Inc.

Suave® is a registered trademark of Unilever Group.

Sue Bee® is a registered trademark of Sioux Honey Association.

Tide® is a registered trademark of Procter & Gamble.

20 Mule Team Borax® is a registered trademark of The Dial Corporation.